Why and where are animals endangered?

Bobbie Kalman

Crabtree Publishing Company

www.crabtreebooks.com

All About Animals Close-Up

Dedicated by Bobbie Kalman and Peter Crabtree
For our friends
Mike and Susan Livesey.
It's fun to paint and party with you.

Author and editor-in-chief
Bobbie Kalman

Publishing plan research and development
Reagan Miller

Editor
Kathy Middleton

Proofreader
Crystal Sikkens

Design
Bobbie Kalman
Katherine Berti
Samantha Crabtree (logo)

Photo research
Bobbie Kalman

Prepress technician
Samara Parent

Print and production coordinator
Margaret Amy Salter

Photographs and illustrations
Wikimedia Commons: Harald Zimmer: page 6 (bottom left);
  www.birdphotos.com: page 7 (bottom); Tbachner: page 14;
  Kent Backman: page 17
Cover and all other images by Shutterstock

Library and Archives Canada Cataloguing in Publication

Kalman, Bobbie, author
    Why and where are animals endangered? / Bobbie Kalman.

(All about animals close-up)
Includes index.
Issued in print and electronic formats.
ISBN 978-0-7787-1469-9 (bound).--ISBN 978-0-7787-1474-3 (pbk.).--
ISBN 978-1-4271-7633-2 (html).--ISBN 978-1-4271-7639-4 (pdf)

    1. Habitat (Ecology)--Juvenile literature. 2. Endangered
species--Juvenile literature. I. Title.

QH541.14.K366 2015   j577   C2014-908188-X
                                          C2014-908189-8

Library of Congress Cataloging-in-Publication Data

Kalman, Bobbie.
  Why and where are animals endangered? / Bobbie Kalman.
    pages cm. -- (All about animals close-up)
  Includes index.
  ISBN 978-0-7787-1469-9 (reinforced library binding : alk. paper) --
ISBN 978-0-7787-1474-3 (pbk. : alk. paper) --
ISBN 978-1-4271-7639-4 (electronic pdf : alk. paper) --
ISBN 978-1-4271-7633-2 (electronic html : alk. paper)
  1. Endangered species--Juvenile literature. I. Title.

QL83.K367 2015
591.68--dc23
                                          2014046817

Crabtree Publishing Company
www.crabtreebooks.com   1-800-387-7650

Printed in Canada/042015/BF20150203

Published in Canada
Crabtree Publishing
616 Welland Ave.
St. Catharines, Ontario
L2M 5V6

Published in the United States
Crabtree Publishing
PMB 59051
350 Fifth Avenue, 59th Floor
New York, New York 10118

Published in the United Kingdom
Crabtree Publishing
Maritime House
Basin Road North, Hove
BN41 1WR

Published in Australia
Crabtree Publishing
3 Charles Street
Coburg North
VIC 3058

Contents

Why are they endangered?

Thousands of species, or types, of animals are disappearing from Earth. These endangered animals are close to dying out for different reasons. Most are losing their **habitats**. Some are being hunted for food or body parts. The chart on the right explains the words scientists use to describe how close an animal is to disappearing completely.

Words to know

endangered Describes animals that are in danger of dying out in the wild. The wild is not controlled by people.

vulnerable Describes animals that may become endangered because they are facing certain risks where they live

critically endangered Describes animals that are at high risk of dying out in the wild

extinct Describes animals that have died out, or animals that have not been seen in the wild for at least 50 years

Quokkas are vulnerable because red foxes are hunting them. Red foxes are an **invasive species** in Australia, which means they do not belong there (see page 18).

Snow leopards live high on mountains in Asia. They are endangered because people kill them for their body parts (see page 9).

What do you think?

Name some ways that people cause animals to become endangered.

Giant pandas are endangered animals. Most of these animals live on **preserves**, where they are protected by people (see page 20).

Critically endangered

The animals in this book are all endangered, but the ones on these pages are critically endangered. There are not many of them left in the wild. These animals are in serious danger of becoming extinct.

Amur leopards are among the most endangered wild cats on Earth. There are fewer than 45 alive in the forests of Russia and China. They are hunted for their fur, bones, and meat.

People hunt rhinoceroses for their horns. Black rhinos live in Africa. There are not many of these animals left.

Sumatran tigers live in Asia. Their forest homes are being taken over by farms and cities (see page 12).

The Vancouver Island marmot is the most endangered **mammal** in Canada. These marmots are losing their homes.

Orangutans live on islands in southern Asia. Many babies are taken as pets, and their mothers are killed.

Mountain gorillas live in Africa. They are hunted for their meat, and some catch diseases from people.

Brown spider monkeys live high up in trees in South America. Most of their forest homes have been taken over by cattle ranches.

What do you think?

These critically endangered animals are almost extinct. What are animals that are almost endangered called?

What are poachers?

Many animals are hunted by poachers. Poachers are **illegal** hunters who make a lot of money selling ivory, fur, leather, and other parts of animal bodies. Ivory comes from elephant tusks. It is carved into different objects, as shown on the right. Animals such as leopards and crocodiles are hunted for their fur, skin, or meat.

tusk

These items were carved from ivory. Thousands of elephants are hunted illegally each year for their tusks!

Many leopards are killed for their fur, which is made into coats and other clothing. People also hunt leopards for their bones, meat, and whiskers. In some countries, these body parts are used in medicines.

crocodile leather

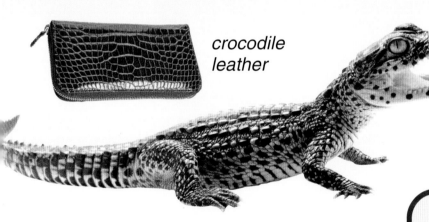

Cuban crocodiles live only in two wild areas on the island of Cuba. They have been hunted for their meat and skin, which is made into leather. These crocodiles are critically endangered.

What do you think?

How can people help these endangered animals by choosing what they buy?

Where do they live?

Habitats are natural places where animals live. Habitats include forests, mountains, grasslands, deserts, islands, wetlands, and oceans. Animal habitats can be found on every **continent** on Earth. As you read this book, make a list of the endangered animals and the continents on which the animals live. Your list will help you do the activity on page 22.

Mountains are tall, steep areas of land. Some are rocky, some are covered in grasses, and some have forests growing on them. Mountain gorillas live in mountain forests in Africa. Snow leopards and Siberian tigers (see pages 5 and 11) live on mountains that are covered in snow in winter.

Forests are habitats covered with trees. Siberian tigers live in different kinds of forests in Asia. Some have snow in winter.

Tropical forests are in areas that are hot all year. Orangutans live in tropical forests in Asia.

People kill lions to protect their farm animals from being eaten by these wild cats.

Grasslands are covered mainly in grasses. Lions live in Africa in grasslands called savannas, which are dry and hot.

Deserts are dry areas that get very little rain or snow. Bactrian camels are critically endangered animals that live in deserts in Asia.

What is habitat loss?

Most animals are endangered because of habitat loss. Habitat loss is damaging or changing natural areas so much that animals lose their homes. Each year, there are more people on Earth, and they need more homes and food. To build homes and grow food, people take over land on which animals live. When animals lose their habitats, they also lose their food and cannot stay alive.

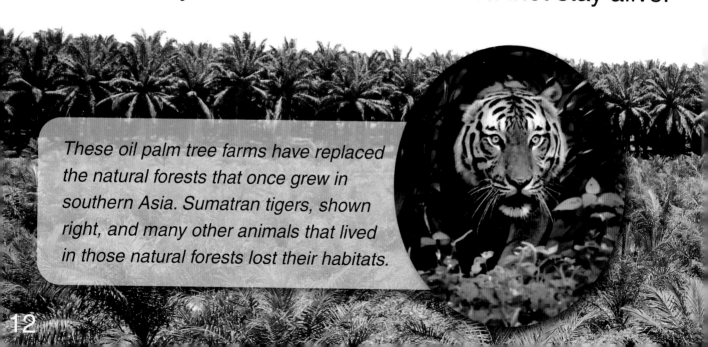

These oil palm tree farms have replaced the natural forests that once grew in southern Asia. Sumatran tigers, shown right, and many other animals that lived in those natural forests lost their habitats.

What are wetlands?

A wetland is a habitat that is covered with water for all or part of the year. Birds, reptiles, insects, and other kinds of animals live in or visit these important habitats, but many wetlands are being drained or **polluted**. Birds that migrate, or fly from one habitat to another, need to stop at wetlands to find food.

Living on islands

Many animals live on islands totally surrounded by water. Madagascar is an island that is part of Africa. Some of the animals on Madagascar are endemic, or found only on that island. Many endemic animals are critically endangered because they cannot be found anywhere else. Endemic animals in danger include the Vancouver Island marmot (see page 7) and the Sumatran orangutan.

AFRICA

Madagascar

Sumatran orangutans live only on the island of Sumatra in Indonesia. They are critically endangered.

Lemurs are endemic to Madagascar. Indris are the largest lemurs. They are losing their forest homes and are hunted by people for their meat. They are critically endangered. These large lemurs are known as "singing lemurs" because they make special sounds that sound like songs. Their songs are several minutes long. The indri on the right is singing.

indri

Black-and-white ruffed lemurs are critically endangered because their forest habitats are almost gone. Without the fruits that grow in these habitats, these lemurs will starve.

What do you think?

These lemurs can be found only on the island of Madagascar. Which endemic animals are critically endangered in Canada and on the islands of Cuba and Sumatra?

Endangered ocean animals

Many kinds of animals live in Earth's five oceans, and many species are endangered. Pollution, **overfishing**, and being hit by boats all pose threats to ocean animals. **Climate change** is another huge threat, especially to animals that live in the Arctic, an area in the northern parts of the continents of North America, Asia, and Europe.

Climate change is causing sea ice to melt. Polar bears hunt seals in the ocean but need to drag them onto ice to eat them. As more ice melts and the pieces float farther apart, it is more difficult for these bears to hunt and eat in their ocean habitat. Polar bears are listed as vulnerable.

Kemp's ridley
sea turtle

The Kemp's ridley and hawksbill sea turtles are hunted for food and for their shells. Both are critically endangered.

hawksbill
sea turtle

The critically endangered Hawaiian monk seals are endemic to Hawaii. They are threatened mainly by pollution and not enough food due to overfishing.

What do you think?

If too many fish die due to overfishing and pollution, what will happen to the seals that eat the fish?

What are invasive species?

*Red foxes are **predators** that hunt many native Australian animals.*

Possums are an invasive species in New Zealand. They eat the eggs and babies of native birds.

Invasive species are types of plants or animals that are brought from one part of the world to live in another. Sometimes these animal "strangers" arrive on ships by accident. Others are introduced by farmers to eat animals or insects that are thought to be pests. Invasive species can cause the numbers of **native** animals to decrease until they become endangered.

Hundreds of unwanted pet pythons have been dumped by their owners into Florida's wetlands. Pythons eat the birds and mammals that are food for native predators.

Gypsy moth caterpillars are invasive insects in Canada. They eat the leaves of over 300 kinds of plants, causing a lot of damage.

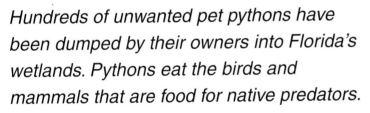

What do you think?

If you were an invasive animal, how well would you adapt to a new home, new foods, or other changes in your life?

Wild pigs are invasive in many countries. They eat any kind of food and can live in many habitats.

19

Living on preserves

National parks and preserves are areas of land where animals are protected. Giant pandas on preserves are fed and looked after by people. Panda cubs are born there. Scientists study these endangered animals and release a few of them back into the wild to see how well they can survive on their own.

Giant pandas live only in China. This worker is taking care of some giant panda cubs at a preserve.

Thousands of elephants and rhinos are killed by poachers each year for their tusks and horns. In some countries in Africa, national parks protect animals. Some national parks have animal orphanages, which take care of baby animals whose families have been killed by poachers. The baby animals are often very sad and need to be held, as well as fed.

What do you think?

Many baby animals lose their mothers. How are the people on these pages taking care of the animal babies without mothers?

Where on Earth?

With a group of friends, draw a huge map or globe of Earth with all the continents on it. Then draw pictures of the endangered animals in this book and place the pictures on the continents where the animals live. Using the books and websites on page 23, do some research on how you can help endangered animals.

Europe
North America
Asia
South America
Africa
Antarctica

Draw the endangered animals that live in...
Africa
Asia (Indonesia, Sumatra, Russia, China, Siberia)
Australia and Oceania (Australia and New Zealand)
North America (Canada, Cuba, Hawaii)
South America

Learning more

Books

Earth's Endangered Animals series.
Crabtree Publishing Company, 2005-2007.

Kalman, Bobbie. *The ABCs of Endangered Animals* (The ABCs of the Natural World). Crabtree Publishing Company, 2009.

Kalman, Bobbie. *Endangered baby animals* (It's fun to learn about baby animals). Crabtree Publishing Company, 2012.

Websites

Animal Fact Guide
www.animalfactguide.com/animal-facts/

What's the Problem: Endangered Animals for Kids
www.sheppardsoftware.com/content/animals/kidscorner/ endangered_animals/whats_the_problem.htm

Endangered Animals Game!
www.sheppardsoftware.com/content/animals/kidscorner/ endangered_animals/endangered_game.htm

Words to know

continent (KON-tn-uh nt) noun One of the seven large areas of land on Earth

climate change (KLAHY-mit cheynj) noun A change in Earth's climate that lasts for a long period of time

habitat (HAB-i-tat) noun The natural place where a plant or animal lives

illegal (ih-LEE-guh l) adjective Against the law

invasive species (in-VEY-siv spee-seez) noun A plant or animal that is not native to an area and causes big problems in its new home

mammal (MAM-uh-l) noun A warm-blooded animal that gives birth to live young

native (NEY-tiv) adjective Belonging to or from a specific area

overfishing (oh-ver-FISH-ing) noun Catching too many fish in one area

polluted (puh-LOO-tid) adjective Made unclean by adding harmful waste

predator (PRED-uh-ter) noun An animal that hunts other animals for food

preserve (pri-ZURV) noun A natural area set aside by a country's government to protect the plants and animals living in that area

A noun is a person, place, or thing. An adjective is a word that tells you what something is like.

Index